50 Years of Phoenix

'Deltic' No 55006 *The Fife and Forfar Yeomanry* crosses the Royal Border Bridge at Berwick-upon-Tweed, on the East Coast Main Line, with 'The Talisman', the 16.00 London King's Cross–Edinburgh service, on 12 June 1976. *John Cooper-Smith*

50 Years of Phoenix

Celebrating 50 years of the Phoenix Railway-Photographic Circle

Edited by Jim Knight & Wyn Hobson

Silver Link Books

First published in 2021

British Library Cataloguing in Publication Data

A catalogue record for this book is available from the British Library.

ISBN 978 1 85794 591 1

Silver Link Books
Mortons Media Group Limited
Media Centre
Morton Way
Horncastle
LN9 6JR
Tel/Fax: 01507 529535

email: sohara@mortons.co.uk
Website: www.nostalgiacollection.com

Printed and bound in the Czech Republic

Contents

Front cover: Northern Trains CAF-built unit No 195128 passes through Grange-over-Sands, on the Cumbrian Coast Line, on 6 March 2020. *Nigel Capelle*

Back cover: A Class 91 on a southbound East Coast Main Line service at Eaton, south of Retford, Nottinghamshire, is silhouetted against a colourful sky just after sunset, 21 November 2012. *Steve Arthur*

Foreword by Jim Knight, Co-Editor, and Chair of the Phoenix Railway-Photographic Circle

It is my great pleasure to present this book on behalf of the Phoenix Railway-Photographic Circle (PRPC). Though it is PRPC's first book for some 40 years, the Circle has gone from strength to strength in the interim, and as we celebrate the 50th anniversary of the Circle's formation in 1971 it is an appropriate moment to share a representative selection of images by members both present and past.

Our three previous publications appeared in the 1970s and early 1980s. There are 35 current members of the PRPC, and all of them, together with some former members, have contributed images for this book – there are more than 50 contributors in total. My thanks are due to current and former members alike for allowing their work to be included.

The creation of the PRPC is explained in the opening chapter. A. Wyn Hobson, founder and now Life President of the Circle, recounts the story, which is illustrated with images taken by members in the 1970s and early 1980s. The themed chapters that follow present images from across the half-century; they will hopefully stimulate thought and ideas in the reader. Each image is captioned and credited.

Many thanks are also due for the knowledge and assistance provided by Wyn during the process of image selection and the publishing of this book, and for the support of the editorial team, Martin Higginson, Russell Saxton and Dafydd Whyles.

The PRPC continues to be a vehicle for promoting alternative approaches to railway photography, in order to explore setting, circumstances, and detail concerning the operation of railways. While the Circle is predominantly formed of members from the UK, we also benefit from the input of members from other countries, who add to the variety of scenes captured, and provide a welcome opportunity to engage with colleagues across the world.

Taking photographs of railways is not a difficult task. Producing memorable and striking images, however, is a different matter. The digital world offers much to the present-day photographer, and a profusion of advances have been, and are being, made in camera technology and post-production software.

The processing of images, often performed with limited resources in the darkrooms of the past, or dependent upon the efforts of a photo lab outside the photographer's control, can now be performed entirely by the photographer. Thus, the skill-sets and innovation needed to create ever more revelatory pictures are constantly evolving. I believe we should continue to push the boundaries of railway photography, and our final chapter covers some of the latest work by members – a presentation of recent alternative compositions, use of modern technology, and new processing techniques.

We hope you enjoy this book. Please do visit our website, which is regularly updated with new images, at www.phoenix-rpc.co.uk.

Jim Knight
March 2021

Chapter 1: Promoting alternative railway photography by Wyn Hobson, founder of the Phoenix Railway-Photographic Circle

The Phoenix Railway-Photographic Circle was the product of a time of change. The end of steam traction on British Rail, in 1968, had left many railway enthusiasts feeling that there was very restricted scope for pursuing their hobby. Among the majority, there was little or no enthusiasm for the diesel and electric traction that had taken over rail services; and few photographers felt that turning their cameras towards the new types of motive power was worth their time and money.

Since 1967 I had been a member of the Railway Photographic Society, a long-established circulating-portfolio group, and by early 1970 it was clear to me that its portfolios contained less and less new work (mostly depicting industrial or overseas steam), and more and more shots from the 1950s and early 1960s that in pre-1968 days would not have been considered to be of a high enough technical standard for inclusion. To the majority of members, anything was preferable to photographing diesels.

English Electric Type 4 Nos 412 and 419 pass Dallam, just north of Warrington, with the 14.00 Glasgow Central–London Euston train on 22 March 1971. *John Cooper-Smith*

I had the idea of setting up a new circulating-portfolio society, to bring together photographers actively interested in diesel and electric traction. A further aim stemmed from the other major change affecting UK railway photography in the 1960s. This had begun with the publication of Colin T. Gifford's ground-breaking album *Decline of Steam* in 1965, followed by two photo-features under the title 'The New Approach' (curated by Ian Krause) in the magazine *Railway World*, and by the album *Steam Portfolio*, edited by Geoffrey Kichenside, which appeared in 1968. The photography explored unconventional viewpoints and composition, unusual combinations of light and shade, and varied juxtapositions of trains and the surrounding environment, in a variety of weather conditions – thereby presenting an enriched record of the ways we saw steam traction in its last years in Britain.

In the spring of 1970 I was in the middle of what today would be termed a gap year, doing clerical work in London. I contacted another recent recruit to the Railway Photographic Society, John Cooper-Smith, then a student at one of the big London teaching hospitals, and put to him my idea for a new society. At first he inclined more towards exploring the possibility of setting up a new section of the RPS, rather than a completely separate entity; so I put that proposal to Maurice Earley, the founding Secretary, offering to run the new section for him if he wished. He, however, was unwilling to create a further complication in what was already a logistically

It is Christmas Eve 1967, and snow is falling at Sheffield Midland station as Class 45 No 101 (which became 45061 under the British Rail TOPS locomotive class renumbering system adopted in 1973) gets the road for a relief working to London St Pancras. The steam escaping from the heating system adds to this atmospheric scene. *Les Nixon*

complex operation, with three geographically separate circles that also circulated inter-circle portfolios. So, with John Cooper-Smith in agreement, I decided to go it alone.

In the late summer, as I prepared to return to university, I circularised just over 60 photographers who had had photographs of diesel and electric traction published in the three leading UK railway enthusiast magazines over the previous few years, inviting them to join a new photographic society that would be specifically concerned with the photography of modern (i.e. non-steam) forms of railway traction. I expressed the view 'that such a society could have a major role to play in fostering this branch of the art, since its practitioners are few relative to the total number of railway photographers, and since the railway journals tend to confine themselves to reproducing pictures which have news-value, as opposed to photographs of a pictorial or experimental nature.'

In a circulating-portfolio system, the box that forms each portfolio is sent by post from member to member round the whole circle or a section of it; each member enters a specified number of prints (having extracted those prints of his that are returning to him after completing a round), and writes comments on his fellow members' entries on the criticism-sheets provided. Further comment and discussion are carried on in a notebook. Submitting one's work for comment and analysis by others, however, is not something that appeals to everyone; thus it was a group of 14 photographers who came together in 1971 to form the Phoenix Railway-Photographic Circle.

By the end of the year, members' thoughts were turning towards the idea of producing a photo-feature to be submitted to the magazine *Modern Railways*, and this appeared in the December 1972 issue, generating a small handful of applications to join the Circle. Meanwhile, nine members decided to set up a portfolio for the circulation of colour transparencies, and this started on its first round in the same year.

Our ambitions next coalesced around the idea of producing a whole book of diesel and electric rail traction photography. This presented a much greater challenge: hitherto, no book of that kind had been published in the UK. Which publisher could be persuaded to shoulder the attendant risk? The answer came, unexpectedly, in 1973, when a publisher in Truro brought out a 96-page volume entitled *Diesels on Cornwall's Main Line*, to join a dozen or so books of steam traction photography already produced or projected. We

Above right: No D1001 *Western Pathfinder* is stabled at Westbury traction maintenance depot on the evening of 7 November 1975. *Geoff Gillham*

Right: It is 10.40 on 28 March 1973 at London's King's Cross station, and 'Deltic' No 9016 *Gordon Highlander* erupts. The locomotive will reverse the length of the station and cross the complicated pointwork to access the King's Cross fuelling point. The identity of the foreground 'Deltic' was not recorded. *Peter Shoesmith*

swiftly threw our hat into the ring, and the upshot was the publication of *Modern Rail Album*, edited by me for the Phoenix Railway-Photographic Circle, in 1974. A second album, *BR Diesels and Electrics around Britain*, followed two years later.

Each of our ventures into print led to a further increase in membership. This, and the financial and other considerations attendant on producing complete volumes, made it advisable for us to institute a system of Annual General Meetings, to discuss and agree current projects and ideas for new ones; our first such meeting was held in Birmingham in November 1974. It was also agreed to hold future AGMs in the spring, and to meet less formally in the autumn, by invitation of a different member each year, at his home. In due course, these latter meetings came to include a prearranged visit to a railway site, such as a traction maintenance depot, to explore photographic possibilities.

By now, three priorities had emerged among the growing membership of the Circle. Some pursued the aim of developing new pictorial approaches to the photography of modern traction. Others, conscious that their interest in photographing diesels and electrics made them a small minority among the remaining UK railway enthusiasts, had leapt at the chance of becoming part of a society of like-minded practitioners. In both groups, there were several who saw the Circle as a way of getting their photographic work into print, and who were very focused on publication.

Experimentation with non-conventional

No 33002, working the 10.10 Bristol Temple Meads-Portsmouth train, is framed in one of the arches of the Kennet & Avon Canal aqueduct, near Bradford-on-Avon, on 4 July 1983. *Geoff Gillham*

On 15 July 1975 'Deltic' No 55003 *Meld* accelerates past Belle Isle, on the climb out of London's King's Cross, heading towards Copenhagen Tunnel, while a Class 31 descends towards Gasworks Tunnel and the terminus with an outer-suburban commuter service. Meanwhile, a Class 501 DC electric multiple unit passes above on the North London Line, working a Richmond-London Broad Street service. *John Glover*

A Class 45, heading a Sheffield-London St Pancras express on the Midland Main Line, passes the impressive semaphore signal gantry at Cricklewood as it nears its destination in May 1978. *Les Nixon*

approaches made a rather hesitant start (most of the pictures in our 1972 photo-feature were fairly middle-of-the-road by today's standards), but slowly gained ground in the Circle's portfolios; moreover, *BR Diesels and Electrics around Britain* embodied a further move away from the traditional sunlit front-three-quarter view. In the years immediately following its publication, we searched for an opportunity to produce a larger book of photographs, on paper of better quality, and if possible including colour work. The prospect of interesting publishers in this last objective remained remote, given the costs involved; also, finding a theme that would maximise the scope for pictorial innovation while attracting the general railway enthusiast was a problem that generated much discussion. At length, however, we learned that a long-established and prestigious publisher was developing a transport list for the first time, and in due course our book proposal to them was accepted – albeit containing black and white photography only.

Trains of Thought, published in 1981, represented a considerable advance on our previous publications, both in artistic terms and as regards quality of production. The volume received favourable reviews, including one in the *Times Literary Supplement*. However, it was not a commercial success. The UK publishing industry was moving into a period of recession and retrenchment, and the publisher lacked the financial resources to expand its sales effort into specialist railway enthusiast outlets.

The long-term result was that other publishers remained nervous of publishing albums of primarily pictorial modern-traction photography. The way the market for books on diesel and electric traction was developing was an important influence in this regard: the trend in the 1980s was towards albums whose captions were very substantial, embracing

No 47420 is framed by two ex-Great Western Railway lower-quadrant signals as it leaves High Wycombe with the 17.42 Birmingham New Street– London Paddington service on 12 April 1980. *John Vaughan*

detail on mechanical and engineering features, service patterns and performance, and relevant historical matters. The function of the photographs was to illustrate the factual content, and nothing more. Pictorial photography – which one of our founder members defined as a picture that shows not only the subject, but also what the photographer feels about it – was off the agenda.

Our response was to diversify into other outlets. There were more magazine photo-features under the Phoenix banner, most notably in the short-lived *Railway Photography & Video* (October/November 1986 – including, at last, some of our colour work, as well as substantial extracts from members' criticism-sheet comments on the photographs reproduced); the American *Trains Illustrated* (May 1991); *Railways Illustrated* (January 2004 – an all-colour selection); and *Rail Express* (December 2016 – another all-colour selection). Phoenix members also continued to contribute individually to books and magazines, occasionally succeeding in getting less conventional images into print. Members contributed pictures to a publication by the Institution of Railway Operators in the early 2000s.

In the new century, we reached a wider public audience by means of exhibitions. The first was held at the National Railway Museum in York (2005-06), moving to the Scottish Railway Museum, Bo'ness (2006-07), then to Pecorama, Devon (2008-09); we also mounted a series of well-received exhibitions at the 'Brief Encounter' museum in Carnforth railway station (2012, 2014, 2016 and 2019, with another projected for 2021).

Without a doubt, however, the most important development in the PRPC's first half-century was the arrival of digital photography. The technology made it possible to take almost limitless numbers of images, then delete those not wanted at the press of a button, without incurring the expense that a similar proceeding would have entailed with celluloid film. Colour photography became almost as cheap as black and white, and the increased ISO speeds that became available opened up extensive possibilities of photographing moving trains in low-light conditions such as twilight. As a result, experimentation became easier, and the PRPC substantially widened its exploration

No 50019 *Ramillies* is seen approaching Banbury with the 11.30 London Paddington–Birmingham New Street service on 28 February 1981. On the left is Banbury South signal box, which continued in use until 2016. *John Vaughan*

A hybrid two-car diesel multiple unit forming a stopping service is framed by a bracket semaphore signal as it approaches the station at Penmaenmawr, on the North Wales Coast main line, on 28 July 1975. *Wyn Hobson*

A pair of Class 37s hauling a train of steel coil, probably heading for Corby Steelworks, stir the interest of passengers at Melton Mowbray in October 1985. *Peter Shoesmith*

of pictorial possibilities in railway photography.

The first print of a digital image was placed in a Phoenix portfolio in 1996. The Circle's first website was created in 2004 and an online gallery of members' work, accessible to the public and including digitised selections from the box portfolios, was created in 2007. A separate online gallery, accessible to members only and enabling comments to be added, was started at around the same time; and in 2011 this became

a fully-fledged online parallel to the portfolios of prints and transparencies, eventually superseding the transparency section. It also made it easier for non-UK-based photographers to become members and participate in some of the Circle's activities. Also around this time, Facebook and Flickr groups were created, to expand online awareness of the PRPC and its work.

Digital technology has also had an effect on methods of publication, making small print-runs economically

It is 09.05 on the bright, cold morning of 6 December 1980 as the low winter sun catches No 25043 and its train in bay platform 4B at Crewe station. Parcel trolleys abound, and a couple of AC electric locomotives wait to ply their trade out on the main lines. A guard strolls along the platform, his duties perhaps complete for the time being. *Wyn Hobson*

feasible to an extent that was not possible with traditional printing techniques. Since 2016 we have availed ourselves of the services of small digital printing companies to produce calendars using some of our members' best work, and an occasional Journal containing photography and articles by members. An internal 'Photographer of the Year' competition contributes material to both

publications. The Journal is also available as a free online download; the first issue attracted just under a thousand takers.

At the end of its first 50 years the Phoenix Railway-Photographic Circle operates in an aesthetic climate that is perceptibly different from the one that existed in the railway enthusiast world at the time of its founding. The enthusiast magazines regularly publish

photo-features that present artistic approaches that would have been anathema to most survivors of the end of steam traction in 1968.

Moreover, this variety is not confined to photographs of diesel and electric traction: in contemporary steam-train photography, also, there is a growing search for new juxtapositions of train, environment and light.

At the PRPC's 2015 Annual General

A London Underground 'C Stock' train approaches Ladbroke Grove station, on the Hammersmith & City Line as a Hammersmith-Barking service on 15 March 1982. The former Great Western Railway signal box is just visible on the right, with the A40(M) road beyond. Tower blocks of the Silchester Estate, North Kensington, dominate the backdrop. *John Glover*

This group photograph was taken on John Vaughan's camera by a passing railwayman during a Phoenix visit to Hither Green traction maintenance depot in South East London on 9 October 1982. Some of those pictured have contributed to this book; they are John Vaughan, Colin Marsden, Brian Morrison, John Glover, John Whitehouse, Kevin Lane, Les Nixon, Peter Shoesmith, Geoff Dowling, Philip D. Hawkins and Wyn Hobson.

Meeting, a small majority voted to allow the submission of steam traction photographs in the members-only online galleries, on a trial basis for a year. Entries were to be limited to one per member in each gallery, and were to adhere to the Phoenix ethos of being 'more visually interesting than the conventional front-three-quarter shot'.

The 2016 AGM agreed to run the experiment for another year, and at the 2017 AGM it was resolved to make the new arrangements permanent. I pointed out that the original ban on steam photography had been imposed to prevent the presenting of mediocre steam traction photographs from members' archives, in preference to engaging with the modern scene. The need for this precaution had by now disappeared.

Our search for new views of trains in landscapes of all kinds thus continues, on a broadened basis, forward into the next half-century. In the meantime, this chapter showcases some of the founding members' work from the first few years of the Circle.

Subsequent chapters are themed, and look at different techniques that members and former members have employed to achieve images of quality. The final chapter looks at recent images from members, which push the boundaries of composition, processing and use of modern technology; brief explanatory summaries accompany these photographs.

During the Hither Green visit of 9 September 1982, Wyn Hobson is seen in an engine shed pit (by permission) photographing a pair of Class 33s. *Peter Shoesmith*

Chapter 2: Into the light

For many enthusiasts, the optimal conditions for photographing a train are those in which bright sunlight reflects off both the nose and the side of the train (a 'sun over the shoulder' front-three-quarter view). In Britain, however, such conditions are only occasionally available. And memory (the object of all photography) can be stimulated by an infinity of variations in the elements of light – direction, angle, quality, intensity and colour. Light determines more than the degree of brightness or darkness in a photographed scene: it can also serve to call forth recollections of atmosphere and mood, season and time of day. Some of the most dramatic effects can be produced by shooting towards the light source, emphasising glow, silhouette, shadow or light flare. Some fine examples are included in this chapter.

The winter sun is rising from behind the Alcan loading facility at North Blyth, on the north-east coast of Northumberland, and GBRf's No 66737 *Lesia* has just drawn forward from the plant with 12 PCA tanks loaded with alumina, part of the consist that will make up the early morning departure to the processing plant at Fort William, in the West Highlands of Scotland, on 8 December 2018. *Stephen Veitch*

As the early morning mist rises from the fields alongside the River Caldew on 27 March 2012, a Northern Rail Class 156, forming the 06.30 Whitehaven–Carlisle service, passes the Stead McAlpin textile mill in Cummersdale near Carlisle. *Gordon Edgar*

No 40149 is working hard with a loaded coal train as it climbs away from Mills Hill, Greater Manchester, on the former Lancashire & Yorkshire main line, on 20 November 1975. Meanwhile No 40019 drifts down grade with a rake of empties. *David Flitcroft*

No 50002 *Superb* restarts the 07.14 Glasgow and Edinburgh to Penzance train from Truro on 10 September 1987. *Stephen Dance*

No 37418 *An Commun Gaidhealach* skirts Erbusaig Bay, near Kyle of Lochalsh, with the 17.00 Kyle of Lochalsh–Inverness service on 29 August 1990. *Mark Lawrence*

The signalman is silhouetted in his box as dawn breaks at Brundall Junction on the Wherry Lines, between Norwich and the coastal ports of Lowestoft and Great Yarmouth, on 5 January 2012. *Ian Dinmore*

A Freightliner container train hauled by No 66564 cuts through the early morning mist over the flood plain of the River Tame at Lea Marston, Warwickshire, on 19 August 2011.
Andrew Maycock

No 66426, with No 66420 at the rear, approaches Wymondham South Junction with a Norwich-bound Breckland Line railhead treatment train (RHTT) on 23 October 2009. This is a circular working that starts and finishes in Stowmarket, Suffolk; Sandite is being sprayed on the rails to lessen the risk of service trains slipping during the leaf-fall season. *Dave Pearce*

On 28 October 2018 Nos 37059 and 37218 (nearest the camera), powering a Carlisle to Alnmouth and return railhead treatment train, accelerate through Stocksfield, Northumberland, with exhaust, spray and leaves flying in the low afternoon light. *Stephen Veitch*

Abellio Greater Anglia No 156407, forming a Great Yarmouth–Norwich service, heads along misty Broadland rails towards Acle, Norfolk, on 12 March 2014. *Steve Arthur*

Chapter 3: Sight lines

A favourite device to make an image stand out from the crowd is the use of leading lines. This can be achieved by using a composition technique that features linear shapes, such as a road, river, fence-line, or indeed railway lines, carriages or wagons. The goal is to lead the viewer's eye through the picture to the intended subject. We instinctively follow these lines to see where they go.

The type of leading line used can change the impact of an image considerably. Horizontal leading lines are often associated with calm and tranquillity. The wide nature of a shot can convey openness, and can be especially atmospheric when paired with good light. Vertical lines are often used to convey power and strength. Diagonal lines can provide a sense of change, motion or direction; where the eye is drawn downward, calm is suggested, while lines sloping upwards tend to add unease and tension when framed well.

With the Lake District mountains as a backdrop, an unidentified DRS Class 88 descends from Shap Summit towards Penrith with a Daventry–Mossend 'Tesco Express' container train on 24 February 2018. This working, which runs regularly six days a week, is one of the longest regular freight trains in the UK. *Bob Avery*

On 5 June 2019 No 170452, forming the 11.39 Glasgow Queen Street–Aberdeen service, slows for the approach to Arbroath during a wet summer lunchtime. *Stephen Veitch*

Yard pilot shunter No 03180 is seen in Meyer-Newman's scrapyard at Snailwell, near Newmarket, Cambridgeshire, on 18 January 1986. It was one of three present in the yard that day; two of them, including No 03180, are now preserved. *Dave Pearce*

Left: Class 45 No 93 (which became 45057 under British Rail's TOPS locomotive renumbering system) reaches the summit of the Lickey Incline at Blackwell, Worcestershire, with the 08.20 Plymouth–Leeds train on 27 February 1974. *Philip D. Hawkins*

Right: No 380102 descends the single-track branch towards the terminus at North Berwick with a service from Edinburgh on a sunny autumn evening, 15 October 2018. *Stephen Veitch*

A Docklands Light Railway Class B2007 unit heads eastwards at West Silvertown, on a Sunday afternoon service to Woolwich Arsenal, London, on 10 March 2019. *Nigel Power*

At Chillington Wharf, on the outskirts of Wolverhampton, a 'Pendolino' passes as an empty stock working heading to Birmingham New Street on 28 February 2016. *Stuart Hassell*

Class 150 'Sprinter' unit No 150101 approaches Dawlish station as the 12.13 Paignton-Exmouth service on 26 November 2017.
Geoff Gillham

A London Midland corporate-liveried handrail leads the eye to a Class 323 electric unit arriving at Bescot Stadium, forming a service bound for Walsall, on 16 April 2016. *Jim Knight*

A London Northwestern Railway Class 350 'Desiro' electric multiple unit has just left Rugeley Trent Valley station, forming the 06.55 Northampton–Crewe service on 25 April 2018. *John Whitehouse*

An unidentified Class 66 is held in Elford Loop, Staffordshire, with a loaded fuel-oil train from Immingham, Lincolnshire, to Kingsbury, on the outskirts of Birmingham, on 10 January 2012. The colour-light signal and light trails from a passing train, captured by a long camera exposure, illuminate the tankers. *Andrew Maycock*

Chapter 4: Landscape

It may seem simple: see a stunning landscape, point the camera and shoot. But more often than not, you get home, review your handiwork, and the resultant image looks flat and boring. There is more to successfully photographing a landscape, or indeed a landscape that includes a train, than might immediately spring to mind. Your eye will scan an image and selectively focus on the elements you find appealing; the field of vision will encompass a great deal of the scene. Unlike a camera lens or sensor, the combination of eye and brain will ignore everything but the most alluring details within an image, so your camera does need some help.

Generally, photographing landscapes will mean using a small aperture (i.e. a high 'f' number) to maximise depth of field, but this isn't always the case: sometimes a restricted depth of field will enhance an image. Choosing a focal point, using foreground interest, considering the sky (or even excluding it), use of light, leading lines and horizon placement, and your chosen point of view, are all important considerations towards achieving good results.

Amtrak's Train No 5, the westbound 'California Zephyr' (Chicago to Emeryville for San Francisco), crosses the lunar landscape of Solitude, Utah, on 6 September 2018. This picture is a panorama made up of two photographs. *Chris Davis*

No 66532 heads a Crewe Basford Hall–Felixstowe container service along Twenty Foot River, near Whittlesey in the Cambridgeshire Fens, on 8 April 2007. On this day some of the container workings ran on this route instead of via London, due to engineering work on the Great Eastern main line. *Kim Fullbrook*

In November 2009 the Cumbrian coast suffered major flooding during and after a storm. The two road bridges and a footbridge over the River Derwent in Workington were rendered impassable, and road travel between Workington and Maryport consequently entailed a 25-mile detour. The railway provided the only direct link between the two towns, so for six months until May 2010 a free temporary shuttle train service was provided between them. In this view, on 16 April 2010, No 37607 leads the 18.50 Workington–Maryport service past the wind farm at Siddick; No 47501 is on the rear. *Kim Fullbrook*

No 47501 *Craftsman* heads a Workington-Maryport 'Floodex' shuttle service, top-and-tailing with No 37610 *TS (Ted) Cassidy*, as they pass the same wind farm, north of Workington, on 10 December 2009. *Fred Kerr*

On 4 September 2018, viewed from Nethertown, the 15.31 Barrow-in-Furness–Carlisle service winds its way along the Cumbrian Coast, past Coulderton and with St Bees to the north in the distance. No 68005 is leading, with No 68033 on the rear, nearest the camera. *Stephen Dance*

An Anglo-Scottish freight crosses Dent Head Viaduct on the Settle & Carlisle route and is about to plunge into the northern portal of Blea Moor Tunnel. No 66030 is in charge of this Hunterston-Ferrybridge coal working on 11 October 2014. *Richard Jones*

On 24 February 2012 No 66171 works the daily Carlisle Kingmoor-Crewe Basford Hall engineers' service through an idyllic scene, typical of the Settle & Carlisle line. The freight is passing Wharton Dike Farm south of Kirkby Stephen, and is glimpsed from Wharton Lane, which serves the isolated farms at Bullgill and Wharton. *Gordon Edgar*

Viewed from the mountainside high above the town, No 37124, with a loaded coal train, sweeps into Pontypridd station from the Abercynon line, heading for Radyr on 10 June 1982. *Colin Marsden*

On 6 February 2018 a wintry scene greets the approach of a Northern Rail Class 158 diesel multiple unit at Helwith Bridge, on the Settle & Carlisle line, with the River Ribble in the foreground. *Rod Smith*

No 66149, heading a Cottam-Immingham train of coal empties, passes North Leverton windmill, with West Burton Power Station as a backdrop, on 19 September 2012.
Michael Rhodes

A Virgin Trains 'Pendolino', working a London Euston to Manchester Piccadilly service, runs alongside the Trent & Mersey Canal at Salt, Staffordshire, on 10 February 2017.
Scott Turner

Chapter 5: Bridges

Just like railway photographers, bridges come in all shapes and sizes – from large and well-known viaducts to tiny culverts, over- and under-bridges, structures in metal, brick, stone, concrete and wood – not forgetting non-railway bridges that are near the line and can make a useful addition to a railway photograph. Most of us like to photograph them too, so it seemed appropriate to dedicate a chapter to the subject, with views from all sorts of angles, and varied conditions of weather and light.

Under threatening skies, and viewed from the Mawddach estuary, a Class 158 diesel multiple unit operated by Arriva Trains Wales crosses Barmouth Bridge, on the west coast of Wales, on 9 July 2010. *Rod Smith*

Northern Rail diesel multiple unit No 156475 crosses the still waters of the River Kent at Arnside, South Cumbria, forming a Lancaster–Sellafield service on 10 January 2019.
Terry Callaghan

At Berwick-upon-Tweed, GBRf No 66736 *Wolverhampton Wanderers* crosses the River Tweed on the Royal Border Bridge (completed in 1850) with a northbound engineers' train on 15 March 2017. In the foreground is Berwick Bridge (or Old Bridge as it is known), the Grade I-listed road bridge completed in 1624. In between is the Royal Tweed Bridge, completed in 1928 to divert road traffic from the Old Bridge. *Brian Newton*

No 37424 (rebranded as No 37558 *Avro Vulcan XH558*) and Inspection Saloon *Caroline* cross Ledbury Viaduct, on the Hereford–Worcester line, in the last light of 14 December 2016. *Adrian Kenny*

A cross-country Manchester–Plymouth service, headed by No 50024 *Vanguard*, passes University station on the outskirts of Birmingham on 26 March 1982, and is reflected in the waters of the Worcester & Birmingham Canal. *Geoff Dowling*

No 66780 *The Cemex Express* climbs the grade at Ramsgreave & Wilpshire, on the Ribble Valley line north of Blackburn, with a Wembley–Irvine tank train conveying china clay for the Caledonian Paper Mill on 4 December 2019. *Nigel Capelle*

A TransPennine Express Class 185 diesel multiple unit crosses Crow Trees Road at Lingards Wood, between Marsden and Slaithwaite, on 3 June 2019, while down below narrowboaters negotiate Lock 31E on the Huddersfield Narrow Canal. *Malcolm Simister*

The 'Toledo Hauler', a Portland & Western Railroad daily short-haul freight, is seen near Elk City, Oregon, USA. This is a loaded trip working taking lumber and paper products from Toledo to Albany. The train is passing through the temperate rain forest of the Pacific North-West on 15 March 2018. *Charlie Dischinger*

Network Rail's HST high-speed test train (powered by Nos 43014 and 43062 *John Armitt*) crosses Porthkerry Viaduct on the Vale of Glamorgan line, with a view of the Bristol Channel beyond, on 12 June 2014. The train had originated at Derby Railway Technical Centre, whence it would return in the early hours of the following morning.
Adrian Kenny

On 31 May 2019, with the Midland Main Line closed for engineering work, trains were being diverted via Corby and Oakham. An East Midlands Trains High Speed Train crosses Welland Viaduct, Harringworth, on the Northamptonshire-Rutland border, forming the 07.04 London St Pancras–Nottingham service. *Nigel Capelle*

Chapter 6: Shadows and silhouettes

Using silhouettes, or shadows cast by subjects within an image – for example buildings, trees, fences, railway stock, and people – can considerably enhance the resulting photograph. Shadows will assist in defining the shape of objects in a picture, and can give a three-dimensional feel to a two-dimensional image, giving depth, or in some cases changing the view entirely.

No D1015 *Western Champion* engulfs a platform end in fumes at London's Paddington station, as two enthusiasts arrive to take pictures of the preserved diesel-hydraulic locomotive on the 'Royal Duchy' railtour to Par, Cornwall, on 5 April 2009. *Steve Arthur*

From the shadowy depths of Manchester Victoria station, where passengers await the arrival of a service to Manchester Airport, a Northern Class 319 departs eastbound and into the light on 25 February 2019. *Scott Turner*

One of the more remarkable through train workings of the early 1980s was 'The European', which operated between the Port of Harwich and Glasgow Central. The train crossed from one side of the country to the other via the Hope Valley route. No 47570 has run round its train and is about to depart from Sheffield Midland station, bound for Harwich, on 10 December 1983. *John Vaughan*

The driver and guard of a London Northwestern Railway semi-fast service from Crewe to London chat while waiting for their train's allotted path south to become clear at Stafford on 4 December 2018. *Nigel Capelle*

Sunlight and shadows on the ramped access to the platforms, and the famous clock, identify Carnforth railway station on the West Coast Main Line, photographed on 26 October 2012. *Dafydd Whyles*

No 47335, hauling empty coaching stock and a guard's van, awaits a clear road on the up fast line at a misty Crewe station on 29 December 1988. *Wyn Hobson*

A Great Western Railway 'Intercity Express Programme' (IEP) Class 802, forming the 14.03 London Paddington–Penzance service, is captured against the setting sun at Stathe, on the Somerset Levels a few miles south of Taunton, on 4 December 2019. *Nigel Power*

On 30 December 2019 the 15.17 Nottingham–Leeds train was held for several minutes at a signal at Engine Shed Junction, Holbeck, just outside Leeds. This image was captured with a tripod-mounted camera and a 10-second delayed shutter release; the figure running toward the camera is in fact the photographer. *Andrew Shenton*

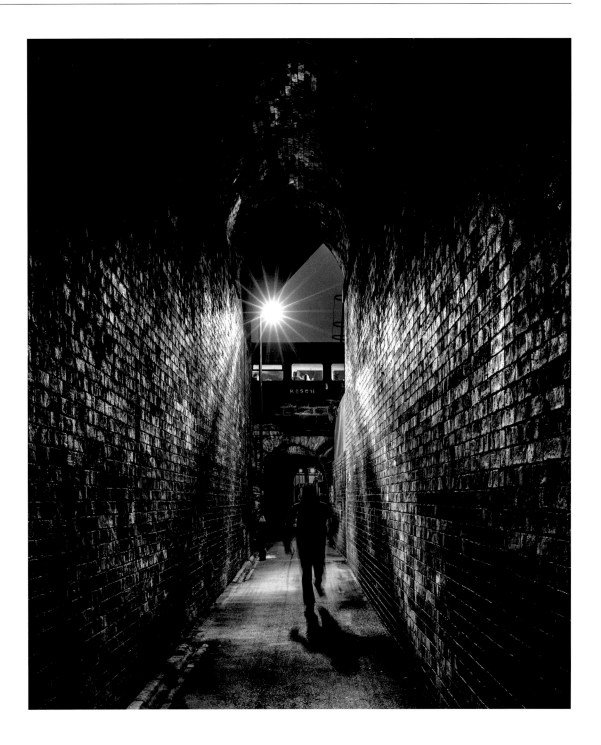

No 66177 takes the station avoiding line at Leicester with a southbound freight train on 20 January 2009. *Russell Saxton*

Stripes and verticals at Rotterdam Centraal railway station, in the Netherlands, on 21 June 2017. In the foreground is a VIRM (or 'Regiorunner') double-deck electric unit of Nederlandse Spoorwegen, while a Railpool Trax F140 electric locomotive and stock glide into the next platform behind. *Nigel Power*

'Pacer' diesel multiple unit No 144011, forming a Manchester Victoria–Leeds service, is balanced by the photographer's own shadow at Todmorden, West Yorkshire, on 20 November 2013. *Steve Arthur*

The previous day's snowfall is yet to thaw as a Class 142 'Pacer' heads east into the early morning sunshine on a cold and frosty day at Healey Mills marshalling yard, Horbury, near Wakefield, on 29 December 2014. *Jim Knight*

Chapter 7: Going Away

Photographs of trains 'going away' rarely represent the most popular choice of angle but, when well composed, and in the right setting and conditions, the results can be very rewarding. The following set of images provides striking demonstrations of this.

A busy moment at Burton Wetmore, Burton-upon-Trent, in the last light of 5 December 2014. No 60017 heads south with loaded oil takers from Humber Refinery, bound for Kingsbury on the outskirts of Birmingham, while heading towards the camera is No 66531 with an East Usk (South Wales) to York empty coal train. Meanwhile, in the yard on the far left is No 66025, about to head a Burton–Southampton container service, and on the next line No 70001 is held at the signal while working a Leeds–Southampton container service. *Phil Grain*

On 3 November 2019 Nos 66956, 66957, 66506 and 66604 pass Gainsborough Trent Junction as a collective 'light engine' working from Whitemoor Yard in March, Cambridgeshire, to their base at Leeds Midland Road, following weekend engineering duties. *Dafydd Whyles*

The replacement driver greets his train, a Class CRH 3 electric multiple unit, at Guangzhou South PDL (Passenger-Dedicated Line) station, China, on 2 January 2012. *Andrew Benton*

A Class 66-hauled empty coal train passes Barnetby, Lincolnshire, on 17 April 2015. In the foreground is one of the impressive array of semaphore signals at this junction, which were replaced by modern signalling the following year. *Steve Arthur*

Light overnight snowfall has yet to clear from the rooftops as No 37065 heads north towards Durham Viaduct on a murky winter's day. The photograph was taken from Red Hills Lane, Durham, on 18 February 1982. *Richard Jones*

An unidentified Class 66 passes Gainsborough Trent Junction and takes the line towards Lincoln with a West Burton Power Station to Immingham empty coal train on 23 April 2014. *Dafydd Whyles*

Another unidentified Class 66 crosses the Ouse Washes at Pymoor, north-west of Ely, Cambridgeshire, with an aggregates train on 26 July 2013. *Martyn Fordham*

Before sunrise on 23 November 2019, a lone bystander watches Northern Rail's No 156482 depart from Newcastle Central station, leaving 'Pacer' No 142012 in its wake.
Robert France

A Class 158 'Sprinter' heads into the depot at Haymarket, Edinburgh, on the morning of 12 January 2018. *Bob Avery*

No 60039 steadies the 08.55 Preston Docks–Lindsey oil train down the grade at Copy Pit, Lancashire, towards the Yorkshire hamlet of Portsmouth on 24 October 2014.
David Hayes

In heavy rain on 30 March 2011, red-liveried 2-foot-gauge 1943-built Motor Rail Simplex four-wheel diesel-mechanical locomotive *Sark* heads a rake of five heavily laden peat cars from 'the moss' for processing at the Bolton Fell Mill at Hethersgill, Cumbria. Visible beyond, on a separate working line, is blue-liveried 1936-built sister locomotive *Lyne*, in charge of one of two other trains awaiting their turn. This was the last peat railway site in England; rail operations ceased here during early summer 2014. *Gordon Edgar*

No 70005 heads a Sunday Crewe–Bristol engineers' train down the steep bank at Marshbrook, south of Church Stretton, Shropshire, on the Marches line on 14 September 2014. *Jim Knight*

No 37426 *Y Lein Fach – Vale of Rheidol* heads the 07.40 (Summer SO) London Euston–Pwllheli train towards Penhelig, near Aberdyfi on the Dyfi estuary, on 30 September 1989. *Wyn Hobson*

Chapter 8: Sunset, twilight and night-time

Photographing moving trains close to, or during, the hours of darkness has become a more realistic option in recent years, given the vast improvement in the ISO capabilities of modern camera equipment. Low-light conditions suggest transition to an alternative visual reality, and make the onset of night a favourite time for some to venture forth to take photographs. A number of PRPC members are particularly adept at low-light photography.

Two silhouetted onlookers are caught in the headlights of an approaching train at Atherstone, Warwickshire, on 16 December 2016. *Scott Turner*

Headlight shining bright in the evening gloom, a London Midland Class 350 electric multiple unit, forming the 17.01 Birmingham New Street–Liverpool Lime Street service, enters the cutting to the south of Coseley station in the West Midlands on 2 December 2017. *Stuart Hassell*

A DB Cargo-operated car transporter train from Halewood to Southampton Docks passes above the Baptist Chapel at Runcorn on 19 April 2017. *Mark Lawrence*

Rush-hour at Ebury Bridge, Victoria, with Battersea power station beyond, on 15 January 2019. *Robert France*

Above: Brush Type 4 No 1595 works a Newton Abbot–Stirling Motorail service through Taunton on 1 September 1971. *John Cooper-Smith*

Left: As a winter's day draws towards dusk, a Cravens Class 105 unit, forming the 16.10 Bletchley–Bedford service, approaches Stewartby on 14 February 1981. The conditions are cold, grey and windless, and the odour of the brickworks hangs in the frosty air. *Geoff Dowling*

Mist sits over the flood plain alongside the River Trent at Gainsborough Trent Junction in this view of 'Sprinter' diesel multiple unit No 150269 working the 07.23 Lincoln–Sheffield service on 28 December 2018. *Dafydd Whyles*

Darkness descends on Tunstead Quarry, Derbyshire, on 5 November 2018 as No 66602 runs past the cement hoppers it has just brought in. Meanwhile No 66607 follows close behind; both are heading for the fuelling point at Great Rocks, near the quarry entrance. *Nigel Capelle*

With the setting sun shining directly down Marsh Lane cutting, to the east of Leeds station, the 16.43 Arcow Quarry–Hunslet stone train passes through, headed by No 66783 *The Flying Dustman*, on 17 July 2018. *Andrew Shenton*

28 December 2018 was the last day for booked Class 37-hauled trains on the Cumbrian Coast line. In the last of the light, No 37424 *Avro Vulcan XH558* is about to depart from Parton, near Whitehaven, with the 14.52 Barrow-in-Furness to Carlisle train. *Robert France*

No 66750 crosses the Hundred Foot Drain at Pymoor, west of Ely, Cambridgeshire, with the Middleton Towers–Goole Glass Works sand train on 15 December 2017. *Jim Knight*

Chapter 9: Glimpsed

The photographers of the images in this chapter have chosen unusual viewpoints in order to reproduce the experience of seeing a subject only briefly or incompletely. Such an approach can lift a fairly ordinary view into a much more interesting one. Compositions of this kind often use foreground interest to frame or add depth to the picture. The effect can be likened to the fleeting glimpse that one might experience while on the move on the railway network, but which, with a camera in hand, one can explore to its fullest potential.

No 37278, seen at Bettws Drift Mine near Ammanford, South Wales, was substituting for a Class 08 shunter that had failed, and which would normally have worked the trip from Pantyffynnon to Bettws, then to Wernos Washery. The photograph was taken from the brakevan of the train, by permission, on 12 June 1987. *Mark Lawrence*

In this view from the signal box at Cargo Fleet Road, Middlesbrough, a Metro-Cammell Class 101 diesel multiple unit is heading towards Middlesbrough from Whitby during April 1983. *Kevin Lane*

A quiet moment in Tunbridge Wells West station booking-hall on 26 May 1984. Class 205 3H diesel-electric multiple unit No 1101 is framed by the window. *Geoff Dowling*

No 25152 with a train of empty parcels vehicles waits at Bangor station, Gwynedd, on 10 August 1983. Suitcases belonging to a large tourist party have been arranged for collection on the opposite platform. *Wyn Hobson*

No 55014 *The Duke of Wellington's Regiment* draws away from Newcastle station with the 07.36 Plymouth–Edinburgh train on 6 June 1981. The 'Deltic' had taken over this service at York. *Richard Jones*

British Rail (Midland) issue bicycle No 8505034, abandoned at Lichfield Trent Valley station together with a discarded BR lamp, sets the scene, typical of the era. A similarly ageing but still in service electric multiple unit, No 304005, arrives as a northbound stopping service on 11 October 1980. *Geoff Dowling*

No 31161 stands on shed at Stratford, East London, on 16 May 1981. *Russell Saxton*

A Southern Trains Class 377 'Electrostar' electric multiple unit is glimpsed on the outskirts of its destination, Brighton, working an East Coastway service from Hastings on 1 May 2004. *Michael Baker*

On 16 January 2019 all is still and everyone has gone to their place of work. A High Speed Train sits in the early-morning quiet of London's St Pancras station, with the slam doors still open. The set had just worked the 05.32 service from Nottingham to the capital. *Robert France*

A train of imported coal, the 06.45 Humber to Radcliffe-on-Trent power station, crosses the swollen River Trent just below the weir at Newark, Nottinghamshire, on 13 March 2015. *Jim Knight*

Hunslet 0-6-0 diesel shunter No 6692, built in 1967, returns 'light engine' to Newdigate Colliery NCB sidings from the exchange sidings on the Coventry-Nuneaton line in March 1978. In the background are wagons formerly used only within the colliery, but now awaiting scrapping. The colliery was closed in February 1982. *Kevin Lane*

Right: A pair of Colas Class 56s on railhead treatment duties roar through Wem, Shropshire, on the last leg of their North Wales and Cheshire railhead treatment train circuit as they head back to Coleham, Shrewsbury, in the late afternoon sun of 2 November 2016. *Nigel Capelle*

Chapter 10: Passengers and bystanders

Railways convey passengers, and capturing these on camera can produce some interesting photographs. There is a definite change in approach to railway photography in many quarters these days, to include human interest and interaction at stations and lineside – far more so than in days gone by when, more often than not, railway photographers would wait to capture a scene devoid of visible human intervention.

No 45103 arrives at Chester with the 11.15 Bangor–Scarborough service on 10 August 1983. *Wyn Hobson*

It is Friday 26 August 2016, a Bank Holiday weekend, and passengers at London's Paddington station are still boarding the 19.03 service to Plymouth, which is already 7 minutes late. *Steve Arthur*

On 22 June 1985 a Class 108 diesel multiple unit sets back into Platform 3 at Stafford station to form a shuttle service for Crewe, during a period of main-line diversions due to station remodelling works at Crewe. *Wyn Hobson*

The erstwhile 'BRUTE' (British Rail Universal Trolley Equipment) often provided a perching opportunity, as seen here at Birmingham New Street station on 30 October 1970, with AC electric locomotive No E3125 in the background. *Philip D. Hawkins*

Skateboarders take advantage of the quiet platforms on a Sunday afternoon at Manchester Victoria on 4 March 1989. This part of the station was originally under the overall roof, but was badly damaged during the Blitz in December 1940, as evidenced by the cut-off roof supports. *David Flitcroft*

No D1023 *Western Fusilier* runs round its train at Birmingham New Street, as two enthusiasts take their photographs. Date unknown, but thought to be 1975. *Peter Shoesmith*

Sunday evening commuters board a local stopping service at Tianjin railway station, China, on 5 September 2010. *Andrew Benton*

Above: Colourful hats and winter boots are in evidence as two seated people watch the trains go by at York station on 29 December 2017. *Martin Higginson*

Left: A family greeting scene observed in August 1988. Glengeary is a commuter station on the southern outskirts of Dublin, Ireland, and is part of the electrified Dublin Area Rapid Transport system. *Michael Baker*

PRPC members Martyn Fordham and Steve Arthur capture the scene at Carlisle station on the evening of 1 October 2012. The Cumbrian rain has played its part in finding the low spots on the platform as Martyn and Steve go about their work. *Gordon Edgar*

Commuters await their train on Platform 5 at Birmingham New Street station on 28 December 2017. The picture is a single frame, utilising the reflections from the double-glazing of the 'Voyager' unit from which the photograph was taken. *Terry Callaghan*

Three lads peer into the cab windows of a High Speed Train set at Swansea station in June 1977. *Les Nixon*

Commuters disembark from a locomotive-hauled Fife Circular service, headed by Direct Rail Services' No 68006 (in Scotrail livery) at Edinburgh Waverley station on 19 January 2018. These loco-hauled services ran via Glenrothes and Kirkcaldy. *Bob Avery*

A lone passenger and a Euston-bound 'Pendolino' set at Wolverhampton station on 29 November 2013. *Russell Saxton*

A pop-up barber has set up shop on a railway bridge at Guangzhou, China, over the Guangzhou–Shenzen and Hong Kong railway line, on 3 January 2012. A CRH Class 1 electric multiple unit passes beneath. *Andrew Benton*

Chapter 11: Staff

Including those who work on the railway adds life and sometimes a story to a photograph. Here are just a few of the many images captured by PRPC members where railway workers are glimpsed going about their daily business of keeping the railways running.

A Class 101 diesel multiple unit passes Llandudno Junction signal box during a guided visit by a university railway club on 23 October 1982. *Wyn Hobson*

No 45059 stands at Saltley motive power depot, Birmingham, in the company of Nos 25256, 47345 and an unidentified Class 47 on 22 May 1975. *Philip D. Hawkins*

Railway staff load mail into the guard's compartment of a Class 104 diesel multiple unit at Leicester station on 5 July 1977. *Martin Higginson*

A comical moment on Penzance railway station as a member of the train cleaning staff appears to have lost control of a broom. Meanwhile, recently arrived Class 52 No 1005 *Western Venturer* sits on the blocks at the Cornish terminus, having arrived with a service from London Paddington, on 10 May 1975. *John Whitehouse*

A long-lost scene of the 'Brighton Belle' being prepared for its next turn of duty at London's Victoria station. This was one of three five-car electric Pullman units built in the 1930s by Metro-Cammell, and was photographed at the London terminus in April 1971.
Michael Baker

Above: Carriage cleaners at Fuzhou depot, China, on 19 February 2010. *Andrew Benton*

Right: A welder carries out repairs as sleet falls during a line possession at the eastern portal of Moffat Tunnel, USA, on 4 May 2001. The tunnel is 6.2 miles long, is equipped with forced ventilation, and was completed in 1927. It is located 50 miles west of Denver, Colorado. *Chris Davis*

A smartly attired crossing-keeper attends to the manually operated level crossing gates at Worstead, between Norwich and Sheringham, East Anglia, on 22 October 1981. *Martin Higginson*

A British Rail driver, silhouetted with his pipe, is buffering up his Class 86 electric locomotive to the stock of a mid-afternoon service to London Liverpool Street at Norwich Thorpe on 11 November 1989. All services were running late that afternoon at Norwich due to a bomb scare on the railway station. *Dave Pearce*

Two railway workers, deep in conversation, stroll across the yard at Saltley motive power depot, Birmingham, where Nos 25269 and 47178 await their next duties on a foggy 2 February 1975. *Philip D. Hawkins*

One of the last duties for the ill-fated Class 17s was the trip workings to and from Bathgate, for local steelworks in the Airdrie and Gartcosh area of central Scotland. In this view, shunting staff are engaged in making up one of those workings at Bathgate yard on 29 September 1971. *Fred Kerr*

A signal lampman goes about his work at Dhuri Junction, in the State of Punjab, Northern India, on 17 April 2018. *Don Gatehouse*

The driver and second man of Rail Operations Group's No 37601 *Perseus* wait for the signal to clear at Worcester Shrub Hill station, en route from Long Marston, Warwickshire, to Northampton on 10 March 2018. *Jim Knight*

Chapter 12: Whatever the weather

Come rain or shine, fog, frost or snow, it is never a bad time to go out and take photographs. Some photographers may leave their camera in the bag if the sun doesn't appear as the train approaches, but it is possible to use adverse conditions to one's advantage. It may be that one needs to think differently about composition, camera settings or viewpoints, which is a good challenge when conditions are less than favourable.

The following images show some challenging, and some not so challenging conditions, but all aim to illustrate a little of the endless variety of weather encountered on railways both in the UK and across the world.

A North East/South West InterCity service, with a BR/Sulzer Type 4 'Peak' locomotive in charge, crosses the River Avon at Eckington, Worcestershire, on 12 December 1981. *Chris Dyke*

On 14 March 2015 a Burlington Northern & Santa Fe (BNSF) mixed freight rolls past the cemetery at Palmetto, Missouri, USA, on the main line from Kansas City to Memphis, Tennessee, and Birmingham, Alabama. The train is bound for Birmingham. *Charlie Dischinger*

No 60076, at the head of the early-running 08.55 train from Preston Docks to Lindsey (Lincolnshire) oil refinery, comprised of discharged bitumen tanks, coasts down the grade past Frosthulme Mill, Cornholme, in the Calder Valley on 19 January 2015. *David Hayes*

Passing beneath the majestic Yorkshire peak of Pen-y-Ghent, on the Settle & Carlisle route, No 66740 heads the Wembley–Irvine Caledonian Paper china clay tanks train near Selside on 23 January 2019. *Martyn Fordham*

Heavy rain is falling at Birmingham New Street on 23 December 1985 as No 47619, newly arrived from Curzon Street Depot with a parcels service for Northampton, is uncoupled prior to running round the train. *Geoff Dowling*

A Cravens Class 105 diesel multiple unit arrives at a snowbound Hellifield station forming a Leeds-Morecambe service on 28 February 1981. *John Whitehouse*

'Deltic' No 9021 *Argyll and Sutherland Highlander* passes Hitchin South signal box and a track gang with the 11.30 London King's Cross–Leeds 'high speed' service (the load being limited to eight coaches) in wintry but bright conditions on 14 February 1971. *John Cooper-Smith*

Left: At 30th Street station, Philadelphia, USA, an electric multiple unit approaches with a commuter service from Princetown in a blizzard in April 1997. The station is a very busy interchange, serving more than 4 million passengers a year. *Michael Baker*

Below: On a wet and windy day at Brundall, Norfolk, in October 2015, autumn leaves are being blown from the trees as a Class 37 awaits the signal to proceed with a Norwich–Great Yarmouth service. *Ian Cowley*

In the autumn rain and gloom of 18 October 2019 GWR IEP (Intercity Express Programme) train No 800308, forming the 15.29 Swansea–Paddington express, passes the Margam BOC plant in South Wales. *Andrew Shenton*

An unidentified Class 143 'Pacer' unit, photographed at Berkeley Marsh, Wiltshire, forms the 07.20 Westbury–Frome service on the foggy and frosty morning of 29 February 1996. *Mark Lawrence*

No 47521 heads the 11.10 Edinburgh-King's Cross train through a misty Retford, Nottinghamshire, on 3 April 1974. *Philip D. Hawkins*

No 90028 heads the 23.50 London Euston-Glasgow and Edinburgh Scotrail sleeper service through the early-morning mist at Scout Green, north of Tebay, Cumbria, on 21 June 2014. *Robert France*

Very damp conditions at Bangor station on the North Wales Coast line, as passengers disembark from a westbound Arriva Trains Wales Class 175 diesel multiple unit on 6 January 2014. *David Flitcroft*

On a wet February day in 2016 in the centre of Brno, Czech Republic, a variety of umbrellas and an approaching tram are in evidence. *Ian Cowley*

Chapter 13: Urban and industrial

A wide variety of images follows, drawing upon both urban and industrial scenes. Photographic opportunities of this kind were much more plentiful in former times, while today rail-served manufacturing industry has greatly dwindled in extent. Coupled with this, the growth of lineside vegetation goes unchecked in large parts of the UK, and the seemingly never-ending onward march of tall security fencing, in both urban and rural locations, means that finding photographic opportunities is becoming a skilled pastime in itself.

A BR/Sulzer Type 2 locomotive performs some shunting at Hednesford exchange sidings, Staffordshire, on 24 November 1970. In the distance on the left, a Brush Type 4 is taking an empty train forward to a colliery further along this then-busy line. On the right, a gas lamp is still in place over the obviously disused cattle dock – a reminder that, as well as being the location of numerous mines, the area was also farmed.
Peter Shoesmith

An unidentified Class 47 hauls the 15.25 Liverpool Lime Street–Newcastle train past the Manchester Ship Canal locks at Irlam on 19 October 1990. *Kim Fullbrook*

In this 2 March 1978 view from the Bagworth & Ellistown station footbridge, on the Leicester to Burton-on-Trent line, a Rolls-Royce-built diesel shunter (Works No 10212 of 1964) is collecting empties from the sidings to return to Nailstone Colliery. Bagworth Colliery is in the background. The Leicester–Burton line was closed to passenger traffic in 1964, but still remains open for freight traffic. *Kevin Lane*

A Class 116 diesel multiple unit has completed its work on the Birmingham Cross-City line and is crossing Garrison Street, Bordesley, on its way back to Tyseley depot on 13 March 1982. *Geoff Dowling*

On 9 September 1988 a couple of local boys wait at the crossing gates in Quay Street, Ammanford, Carmarthenshire, while No 08995 *Kidwelly* moves a set of HAA hopper wagons from nearby Pantyffynnon Yard for loading at Bettws drift mine. The single platform of the long-closed Ammanford station is visible beyond the signal box. The diesel shunter is one of those with a cut-down cab for working the Burry Port & Gwendraeth Valley line, on which there were a number of overbridges with low clearance. *Don Gatehouse*

On 12 September 1973 'Deltic' No D9007 *Pinza* powers up London's Holloway bank with an East Coast Main Line express from King's Cross to the north, while Class 31 No 5800 crosses the bridge over the main line with a single brakevan. *Brian Morrison*

There is nothing here to suggest that this was the first day of public High Speed Train operation on the Western Region, 4 October 1977. On the right, Class 52 No D1009 *Western Invader* leaves Paddington station with a service to Paignton, passing No 47488 and classmate No D1068 *Western Reliance*, which are awaiting their next duties. *Fred Kerr*

The throttle of No 37218, at the head of a South Bank Tees Dock-Daventry intermodal train on 15 March 2020, is opened up at Washwood Heath, Birmingham, as No 66126 waits for clearance to go forward and run round at Duddeston Junction with an intermodal from Daventry to Doncaster i-Port. *Terry Callaghan*

Left: Storm light at Limehouse as a two-car set of B92 stock heads west on the Docklands Light Railway towards the City of London on 28 October 2018. *Nigel Power*

Right: On 24 March 2012 the race is on at Latchford Sidings, Arpley, Warrington, as two Class 60s run round their respective trains. No 60065, on the left, will shortly depart to deliver coal to Fiddler's Ferry power station, Cheshire, while on the right No 60045 will head back to Liverpool Bulk Terminal with the empties. *Kim Fullbrook*

An office block alongside the River Usk in Newport, South Wales, offers a reflected view of No 60015 heading west with the Westerleigh Murco-Robeston Sidings petroleum tanks train on 15 February 2019. *Nigel Power*

'Pacer' diesel multiple unit No 144016 crosses Paddock Viaduct as it nears its Huddersfield destination forming a service from Sheffield on 13 March 2020. *Terry Callaghan*

No 66035 crosses the Leeds & Liverpool Canal with a train of discharged fuel tanks from Neville Hill to Lindsey oil refinery on 13 November 2019. *Michael Rhodes*

Chapter 14: Phoenix into the future

The Circle will always be looking for new ideas and approaches. This chapter showcases some of our more recent images, which explore a variety of angles, compositions and techniques to present new views. To be successful, a photograph of any type needs to create an aesthetic or emotional response in the viewer, and its success may be measured by the durability of that response. We hope that some, at least, of the images presented here or in earlier chapters have a lasting impact, and thereby provide fresh inspiration to photographers.

This chapter includes a number of images that have been produced as composites of more than one image; any such image is so described, including this book's cover image, details of which can be found at the end of this chapter.

The images on this pair of pages make use of the form that is inherent in one or more of the objects depicted. The first uses an ornate wooden barrier, positioned at one end of the north bay platforms at York railway station, to frame the main subject.

The image of 'Azuma' trains at Edinburgh's Waverley station shows that the photographer has investigated lines and shapes as generators of form. Through the simple action of rotating the camera, a striking image has been secured. Distractions from the main subject have been dealt with at the processing stage: the colour of the blue train in the background has been partly desaturated, and an obtrusive station lamp has been digitally removed. These might be considered fairly minor amendments, but can be key to finessing an image for presentation.

No 68022 *Resolution* in one of the bay platforms at York station on 2 March 2019. *Jim Knight*

Two East Coast 'Azuma' IEP units at Edinburgh Waverley station on 28 July 2020. *Martin Higginson*

These two images demonstrate the benefits of using composite image processing techniques. The first features two photographs taken an hour apart and digitally merged, to assist with exposure levels and principally to benefit from incorporating the city lights from the later of the two photographs. The second image is another merging of two photographs, taken only moments apart, to show both trains perfectly positioned.

Not all photographers agree with merging images; some feel strongly that a photograph should represent the actual scene at the time the shutter was released. Others, however, might suggest that creating composite images is a legitimate aspect of the craft of photography – satisfying the photographer's impulse to make an imagined possibility a reality, by applying the expertise entailed in processing two images to produce a seamless result. It is a debate that will probably never be resolved.

A TransPennine Class 802 'Nova 1' unit passes Morley, on the western outskirts of Leeds, working a Newcastle–Liverpool Lime Street service on 29 September 2020. *Andrew Shenton*

On 30 December 2019 No 91129 heads south from Leeds, crossing the Huddersfield line at Copley Hill with the 15.15 service for King's Cross. The TransPennine Class 185 working the 13.54 Liverpool–Scarborough service arrived moments later. *Andrew Shenton*

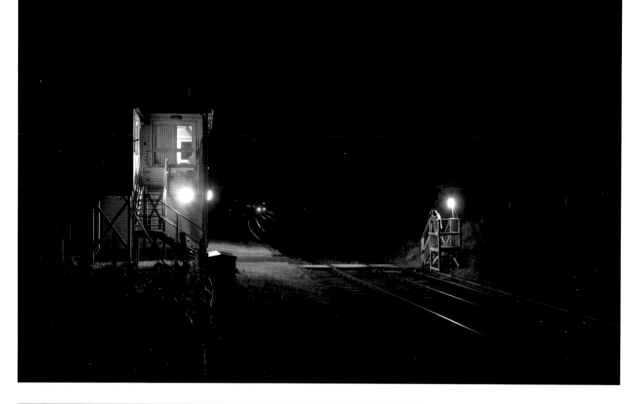

The signaller at Glenwhilley box waits to make a line token exchange with the driver of the 21.03 Stranraer–Kilmarnock service on 7 September 2019. *Robert France*

The seemingly endless advances in camera technology now allow photographs of moving trains to be taken in extremely low-light conditions – which could not even have been considered in the film or early digital eras. The image taken at Glenwhilley was rated at 2000 ISO with a 1/10th of a second exposure. The signaller on the platform is awaiting the arrival of the approaching train, whose driver will hand over a token that allows access to the section of track that the train is about to leave. Simultaneously, the signaller will hand the driver a token allowing the train to access the next section of track.

The image at Gainsborough was taken using 1600 ISO and a 1/25th of a second exposure, and benefits from the atmospheric combination of mist, lights on the locomotive, and those from the signals, including the hint of green from the nearest one, giving the train the right of way to pass through.

Just after 01.00 on 18 September 2020, GBRf's No 66765, heading the Rotherham Masborough–Felixstowe container train, appears through a mist that has risen from the River Trent at Gainsborough. *Dafydd Whyles*

These two images make use of motion blur to great effect. The first combines the motion of the oil tankers crossing the river and the motion of the swirling water approaching the camera. This photograph was taken using a shutter speed of 1/6th of a second, which was enough to give the viewer a sense of the motion of both train and river.

The second image shows a 'Pendolino' running through a station at full line speed, captured using a shutter speed of 1/10th of a second, which was slow enough to add motion blur to the train, contrasting well with the waiting traveller.

A loaded oil train, from Lindsey oil refinery on the Humber Estuary to Kingsbury on the outskirts of Birmingham, crosses the River Trent at Newark on 15 September 2020. *Robert France*

A lone traveller watches as a southbound Virgin Trains 'Pendolino' speeds through Rugby station, on the West Coast Main Line, on 17 March 2019. *Nigel Capelle*

Left: On 14 February 2020, No 70808 rumbles into Carlisle Citadel station with a Carlisle New Yard–Doncaster Roberts Road working, probably taking the wagons (normally used to transport timber) for repair. In the distance, an 'Avanti' 'Pendolino' departs for London Euston. *Stephen Veitch*

Below: Northern Rail diesel multiple unit No 156405, forming a Nottingham–Worksop service, rolls into Shirebrook station on 17 August 2020. *Terry Callaghan*

Reflection images are nothing new, but there is skill involved in capturing them well. As can be seen in the image of a Class 70 at Carlisle, the photographer has used a very low viewpoint, which has made full use of the reflections in the puddle lying on the platform surface.

The second image is quite remarkable, given the considerations that had to be balanced when setting up the shot, including the angle and elevation of the sunglasses, their positioning on the bench to incorporate the water droplets, the point of focus, and the desired depth of field. The limited depth of field helps concentrate the viewer's gaze on the main subject, which is perfectly placed in the lens of the sunglasses.

Left: A DRS Class 68 heads through Cradley Heath with the 16.15 London Marylebone–Kidderminster service on 27 November 2017. *Stuart Hassell*

Below: A CrossCountry Class 220 'Voyager' unit arrives at Birmingham New Street on 24 June 2018. *Stuart Hassell*

Two more low-light images, where the photographer has decided to include motion blur as part of his presentation, but to different degrees. The first, taken at Cradley Heath in the West Midlands, was taken at 1000 ISO, with motion blur well handled at an exposure of 1/20th of a second. The lights from the adjacent bus station have helped here, assisted by the use of a prime lens, always a benefit in low-light conditions.

The second image, taken at Birmingham New Street, is quite different, in that ISO 250 has been selected to reduce grain, but a much longer exposure of 1 second has been employed, to emphasise the motion blur of both passengers and train. Remarkably, it was a hand-held shot, and is testimony to the steadiness of the photographer's grip and also to the vibration-reduction technology available in lenses today.

Left: 'The Art Studio', showing a number of pictures of steam tours out on the main line. *Nigel Capelle*

Right: 'Artwork in Progress': a 'Coradia' Class 175 diesel multiple unit approaches Llandudno Junction, North Wales, forming a Llandudno–Manchester service on 21 March 2019. *David Flitcroft*

Below: 'Artwork in the Field': preserved Norfolk & Western Class 'J' No 611 at Front Royal, Warren County, Virginia, USA, in April 2020. *R. G. Edmonson and Charlie Dischinger*

These photographs depict artwork in various guises. 'The Art Studio' is a collection of photographs of steam tours out on the main line, taken by the photographer then painstakingly superimposed on an art studio scene, using many layers in Photoshop to achieve the result. Each image has also been treated to give it a more painterly effect than that of a photograph.

'Artwork in the Field' is a similarly clever image of an American steam locomotive apparently being caught on canvas in the blink of an eye. The original photograph was taken and digitally edited as a 'part completed painting' by R. G. Edmonson, an acquaintance of Charlie Dischinger. Charlie printed the 'painting' and set it up on an easel in his studio, with lighting to replicate the sun and shadows of the original scene. He then photographed himself 'painting' the scene, and superimposed the result on the original image.

Finally, 'Artwork in Progress' is the combination of a train and some 'sketch' software, which has produced a complex image, complete with pencils and eraser.

And finally...
by Nigel Capelle

The photograph on the front cover of this book is not all it seems, and it is worth recounting how it came about. Using a British Rail-era 'cut-out' 50mph speed limit sign in the cover photograph as part of the title was an idea Jim Knight had after seeing a photograph taken by Terry Callaghan at Grange-over-Sands in Cumbria, incorporating such a sign in the foreground.

A quick search of photo-sharing websites revealed only two other locations with such a sign – not many 50mph cut-out signs still exist, it would seem. I offered to visit all three locations: Grange-over-Sands; Swinderby in Lincolnshire; and Great Corby, just east of Carlisle. However, only Grange presented the possibility we were searching for, and even there a photograph was only achievable from behind the 50mph sign. The only option was to photograph it from that position, combine the photo with a photograph of a passing train, also taken from the rear, and then use computer software to 'flip' the image. After two days and several hundred miles, the picture was duly taken.

Back at home, on the computer, the real work began. First, the image had to be flipped horizontally, so that the 50mph sign was the right way round and the train appeared to be approaching on the correct track. After

correcting converging verticals caused by the low camera position, the image was cropped to omit inessential detail. Because the image had been flipped, all text in the picture was now back-to-front.

The yellow Network Rail sign was flipped horizontally. The multiple unit's number and electronic destination display on the front also had to be flipped horizontally, moving the unit number from the left to the right side and making the destination intelligible. The 'Northern' logo on the side of the train was

digitally removed due to parallax problems, which prevented it from being 'flipped', and the sign on the gable end of the building was cloned out as it was rather distracting. Finally, the 50mph sign was 'painted yellow' using a colour-change tool, then digitally extended so that the book title could be aligned with the '50' and sit comfortably between the top of the train and the upper edge of the photograph. The rest of the book title text was added, and the outcome is as you see it on the front cover of this volume.